FISHES

A TRUE BOOK

by

Melissa Stewart

Children's Press®
A Division of Grolier Publishing
New York London Hong Kong Sydney
Danbury, Connecticut

This spotted garden eel has buried part of its body in the sand.

Reading Consultant
Linda Cornwell
Coordinator of School Quality and Professional Improvement Indiana State Teachers Association

Content Consultants
Ron Coleman, Ph.D.
Jan Jenner, Ph.D.

The photograph on the cover shows a school of French grunts. The photograph on the title page shows a surgeonfish.

Visit Children's Press® on the Internet at:
http://publishing.grolier.com

Library of Congress Cataloging-in-Publication Data

Stewart, Melissa.
    Fishes / by Melissa Stewart.
        p. cm. — (A true book)
    Includes bibliographical references and index.
    Summary: Describes the basic behavior, physical traits, and life cycle of fishes.
    ISBN: 0-516-22038-1 (lib. bdg.)   0-516-25955-5 (pbk.)
    1. Fishes—Juvenile literature. [1. Fishes.] I. Title. II. Series.
QL617.2.S7 2000
597—dc21   99-057543

GROLIER
PUBLISHING

Contents

What Is a Fish?   5

Where Fishes Live   12

A Fish's Body   20

Groups of Fishes   30

Fishes and More Fishes   34

Fishes in Our Lives   40

To Find Out More   44

Important Words   46

Index   47

Meet the Author   48

The beautiful spotted coral cod (top) gets its name from its bright blue spots. When the great white shark (bottom) attacks, it often comes from beneath and behind.

What Is a Fish?

What do you think of when you hear the word "fish?" Do you imagine a brightly colored animal darting through water? Do you think of the fish sticks you ate for dinner last week? Do scary tales of great white sharks come to mind?

The world's salty seas and oceans are full of fishes. You can also find fishes in fresh-water lakes, ponds, rivers, and streams. There are more than 25,000 different kinds of fishes on Earth.

These sweetlips live in the ocean.

The whale shark is the world's largest fish.

Some fishes are very large, and some are very small. A whale shark is longer than two school buses. A dwarf pygmy goby is about the size of the eraser on a pencil.

All fishes have two things in common—a backbone and gills. Your backbone supports your body and helps you move. A fish's backbone does the same jobs.

A fish's gills are like your lungs. When you breathe in air, your lungs help move oxygen into your blood. When water moves over a fish's gills, the gills remove oxygen from the water and move it into the fish's blood.

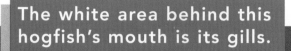
The white area behind this hogfish's mouth is its gills.

gills

Two Fish or

We often add the letters "s" or "es" to make a word plural. But that rule does not apply to words like "sheep" or "deer." When it comes to the word "fish," the rules are even more tricky.

Two masked butterfly fish or two fish

Two Fishes?

A rock beauty and a stoplight parrot fish, or two fishes

You should use "two fish" when you are talking about the same kind of fish, but "two fishes" when you are talking about different kinds of fishes.

Where Fishes Live

Fishes can live in all kinds of places. No matter where a fish lives, it has special features that help it survive. Brightly colored sea horses, moray eels, and clownfish blend in with coral reefs, so enemies cannot see them. Fast fishes, such as marlins, swordfish, and tuna, live

It is hard to see the moray eel because it blends in with its surroundings.

near the surface of the ocean. Each day, they swim many miles in search of food. Most of the fishes that live in deep, dark ocean waters have large eyes and glow in the dark.

These chum salmon (right) are swimming upriver. The African lungfish (below) breathes through its lungs when the water dries up.

Northern pikes can be found in lakes, streams, and rivers. Catfish prefer warm, muddy ponds. A few fishes, such as salmon, move between freshwater streams and the ocean. Lungfish can survive for many months on mudflats.

Fishes come in many different shapes. Some are as flat as a pancake. Others can blow themselves up like a balloon. A few look like lumpy rocks or slithering snakes. Flat fishes, such as flounder and sole, lie on the bottom of the ocean and wait for a meal to come to them. Butterfly fish and angelfish can escape from enemies because their thin bodies fit in tight spaces. Tube-shaped fishes, such as eels, escape enemies or hunt prey by weaving in and out of holes between rocks.

This lumpy-looking longlure frogfish (top) is hiding on a sponge. Predators can see this dazzling emperor angelfish (bottom), but they often have a hard time catching it.

These orange and purple fairy basslets have dark backs and pale bellies.

Many fishes have dark backs and pale bellies. Their backs match the dark water below them, so birds, bears, and snakes hunting from above cannot see them. When otters, sea lions, or bigger fishes look up from below, the pale bellies blend in with the sunlight from above.

A Fish's Body

Most fishes have fins and scales. A fish uses its fins to move in the water. The paired fins help a fish start, stop, and turn. The top and bottom fins help a fish keep its balance and stay still. A fish's tail provides the power it needs to push through

Top fin

Tail fin

Paired fins

Bottom fin

Can you guess how a blue devil damsel fish uses each of its fins?

the water. A fish swims by bending its body from side to side.

The Atlantic sailfish's fins help it to swim at high speeds.

The shape and location of a fish's fins determine how well it can swim. Fishes with slim fins and a narrow tail are fast swimmers. A sailfish's fins help it cruise the ocean at 60 miles (97 kilometers) per hour. Fishes with large, broad fins and a square tail are slower swimmers, but they are better at turning quickly.

Many fishes are covered with scales. The scales over-lap like the shingles on a

Look at this close-up view of overlapping scales.

roof. The scales protect a fish's skin like a suit of armor. A slimy material on top of the scales helps some fishes swim faster and slip out of an enemy's grasp. Special chemicals in the slimy material help a fish fight germs.

Most fishes grow throughout their lives. You can tell a fish's age by counting the number of growth rings on its scales.

Your body temperature is usually about 98.6 degrees Fahrenheit (37 degrees Celsius). Your body works hard to stay at this temperature. If you get too hot, your body sweats. If you get too cold, your body shivers.

Scientists call this warm blooded.
Nearly all fishes are cold blooded.
This means that a fish's body
temperature changes with the
temperature of the water it is
swimming in.

Just like you, a fish has eyes,
ears, and nostrils. A fish can never
close its eyes because it has no
eyelids. Fishes do not sleep like
you, but they do rest by moving
very slowly. Some rest their belly
or side on the ocean floor or a
lake bottom.

This mangrove snapper does not have eyelids. Can you guess what keeps its eyes moist?

Most fishes can taste things with their mouths and with special feelers near their mouths. You can tell what a fish eats by looking at its teeth. Some fishes scrape algae off rocks and coral. Fishes with large, flat teeth can crush the

The sharp teeth of the leopard moray eel show that it hunts other fish.

shells of clams and mussels and eat tough plants. Fishes with sharp, pointed teeth hunt other fishes.

A fish's size can also tell you what it eats. The smallest fishes eat tiny ocean creatures and other fishes' eggs. Most medium-sized fishes eat worms, crabs, shrimp, and smaller fishes. Big fishes eat medium-sized fishes, squid, and other large ocean creatures.

A large koi carp is about to swallow a small goldfish.

Groups of Fishes

Scientists divide fishes into three groups—jawless fishes, sharks, rays, and skates, and bony fishes. Jawless fishes, such as lampreys and hagfish cannot bite food. They have round, sucking mouthparts and slimy skin with no scales. Their skeleton is made of a

This Pacific hagfish is a jawless fish.

flexible material called cartilage. The tip of your nose and your ears are made of cartilage too.

The scales of the blue spotted stingray might look smooth, but they are rough.

Sharks, rays, and skates also have a cartilage skeleton. The rough scales that cover their skin feel like sandpaper. Many of the fishes in this group are good swimmers and ferocious hunters.

Most fishes in the world are bony fishes. Like you, bony fishes have a skeleton made of bone. Carp, tuna, guppies, goldfish, clownfish, and perch are all bony fishes.

Like most fishes, the tomato clownfish is a bony fish.

Fishes and More Fishes

Most fishes begin life when they hatch from an egg. A young fish is called a larva. When it learns to swim, it is called a fry. Some fishes take just a few minutes to become adults. Others take several months or even years.

A salmon fry

Salmon eggs developing and hatching

When it is time for the adults to produce more young, a female lays eggs. Then, a male releases sperm nearby. If an egg and sperm come into contact, the egg will begin to develop. It will hatch a few days or weeks later. A few kinds of fishes, such as guppies and sharks, carry their babies inside their bodies and give birth like people.

Most fish eggs are no bigger than the head of a pin. They may drift in the water, sink to the bottom, or stick to plants or rocks. Many are eaten by other fishes. To make sure that enough young fish will develop, a female fish may lay hundreds of eggs at a time. A female cod may lay more than 8 million eggs a year.

Most fishes do not protect their eggs or care for their young. A few kinds of fishes build nests and guard their eggs. Salmon and trout cover their eggs with gravel. A female sea horse places her eggs in a pouch on the male's belly. A fish called the mouthbrooder

This male sea horse is giving birth.

collects its eggs and carries them in its mouth until they hatch.

Fishes in Our Lives

Fishes play an important role in our lives. People all over the world eat fishes. Their meat is a good source of food. It is high in protein and low in fat. Some people keep fishes as pets. Scientists use other kinds of fishes in experiments.

Baked red snapper makes a tasty meal.

Fishes are also an important part of ocean and freshwater ecosystems. Their eggs are eaten by all sorts of creatures.

When humans pollute water, build dams, or catch too many fishes, they risk destroying the balance of nature.

When people build dams, such as the Hoover Dam on the Colorado River, some kinds of fish may be affected.

Is It a Fish?

Have you ever seen a dolphin or a whale? These animals live in the ocean, but they are not fishes. They are mammals. They do not have gills, so they must come up to the surface for air. They breathe in air through a blowhole on the top of their heads.

   Starfish and jellyfish have the word "fish" in their name, but they are not fishes. Neither animal has a backbone. That is why some people call them "sea stars" and "sea jellies."

These dolphins are mammals—not fishes.

This purple sea star does not have a backbone, so it is not a fish.

To Find Out More

Here are some additional resources to help you learn more about fishes:

 **Books**

Bailey, Jill. **How Fish Swim.** Benchmark Books, 1997.

Ethan, Eric and Marie Bearanger. **Coral Reef Hunters.** Gareth Stevens, 1997.

Hewitt, Sally. **All Kinds of Fish.** Children's Press, 1998.

Landau, Elaine. **Your Pet Tropical Fish.** Children's Press, 1997.

Riccuti, Edward R. **Fish.** Blackbirch Press, 1993.

Richardson, Joy. **Fish.** Franklin Watts, 1993.

Savage, Stephen. **Fish.** Raintree-Steck Vaughn, 2000.

Sneeden, Robert. **What Is a Fish?** Sierra Club Books for Children, 1993.

Organizations and Online Sites

Cool Kid's Fishin'
http://www.ncfisheries.net/ kids/index.html

Find out how to fish safely, learn to identify the parts of a fish, and discover the important role of fishes in the food chain.

Fish Information Service
http://www.actwin.com/fish /index.cgi

Would you like to keep a pet fish? Check out this site before you head to your local pet store. This site also has a list of public aquariums. There is probably one near your home.

Marine Life Learning Center
http://www.fishid.com/

What do fishes eat? How do they stay clean? You can find out all about fishes at this site. See pictures of strange fishes, such as the shortnose batfish and the longlure frogfish.

Sharks and Their Relatives
http://www.seaworld.org/ Sharks/pageone.html

If you are interested in sharks, this site is the place to go. Learn some amazing facts, and see plenty of photos.

U.S. Fish and Wildlife Service Fisheries Program
http://fisheries.fws.gov/

This agency provides many scientists with money to perform important research about fishes and other animals. At this site, you can find out about these programs and learn some interesting facts about fishes that live in your area.

Important Words

algae any of a large group of plants or plantlike things that grow in water

backbone a group of bones that supports your body, helps you move, and protects important parts inside your body

cartilage a flexible material that supports the bodies of some fishes; it also supports your ears and the tip of your nose

cold blooded having a body temperature that changes as air or water temperature changes

fry a young fish that can swim

gill one of the body organs that remove oxygen from water and move it into a fish's blood

larva the first stage in the life cycle of a fish and some other kinds of animals

prey an animal that is hunted by another animal for food

Index

(**Boldface** page numbers indicate illustrations.)

algae, 27
angelfish, 16, **17**
backbone, 8, 43
body temperature, 25, 26
bottom fin, 20, **21**
butterfly fish, **10,** 16
cartilage, 31, 32
cold blooded, 26
coloring, **18,** 19
eggs, 29, 34, 36, **36,** 37, 38, 39, 41
eyes, 13, 26
feelers, 27
fins, 20, **22,** 23
fry, 34, **35**
gills, 8, **9,** 43
great white shark, **4,** 5
groups (of fishes), 30–33
hagfish, 30, **31**
larva, 34

lungfish, **14,** 15
lungs, 8
moray eel, 12, **13, 28**
mouthbrooder, 38
mouths, 27
oceans, 6, **6,** 13, 15, 16, 26, 29, 41, 43
paired fins, 20, **21**
resting, 26
rock beauty, **11**
sailfish, **22,** 23
salmon, **14,** 15, 38
scales, 20, 23, 24, **24,** 25, 30, 32, **32**
scientists, 26, 30, 41
sea horses, 12, 38, **39**
shapes, 15–16
stoplight parrot fish, **11**
tail fin, 20, **21**
teeth, 27, 28, **28**
top fin, 20, **21**
warm blooded, 26
whale shark, 7, **7**

Meet the Author

Melissa Stewart earned a Bachelor's Degree in biology from Union College and a Master's Degree in Science and Environmental Journalism from New York University. She has been writing about science and nature for almost a decade. Ms. Stewart lives in Danbury, Connecticut.